AWESOME ATHLETES

KEN GRIFFEY, JR.

Paul Joseph
ABDO & Daughters

Published by Abdo & Daughters, 4940 Viking Drive, Suite 622, Edina, Minnesota 55435.

Copyright © 1997 by Abdo Consulting Group, Inc., Pentagon Tower, P.O. Box 36036, Minneapolis, Minnesota 55435 USA. International copyrights reserved in all countries. No part of this book may be reproduced in any form without written permission from the publisher.

Printed in the United States.

Cover and Interior Photo credits: Wide World Photos
                                    Allsport USA

Edited by Kal Gronvall

Library of Congress Cataloging-in-Publication Data

Joseph, Paul, 1970-
Ken Griffey, Jr. / Paul Joseph.
      p.   cm. — (Awesome athletes)
Includes index.
Summary: Examines the professional and personal life of the baseball star who plays with the Seattle Mariners.
ISBN 1-56239-639-0
1. Griffey, Ken, Jr.—Juvenile literature. 2. Baseball players--United States—Biography—Juvenile literature. [1. Griffey, Ken, Jr. 2. Baseball players. 3. Afro-Americans—Biography.]
I. Title. II. Series.
GV865.G69J67 1997
796.357'092—dc20
[B]   96-17920
                                                                        CIP
                                                                         AC

Contents

Junior

Not too many people have been around the game of baseball as much as Ken Griffey, Jr. While he was growing up he had the privilege of watching the best baseball players in the world play the game.

As a youngster he would go to the **stadium** with his father, Ken Griffey, Sr. Senior was an **All-Star** outfielder on the Cincinnati Reds. He played with a talented group of ball players called "The Big Red Machine" because they ran over everyone in their way.

On any given day, Junior could be seen taking instructions from Pete Rose, or pitching to Johnny Bench, or taking batting practice from Gary Nolan, or learning to play outfield from George Foster. But most important, he learned the game from his dad, who was always there to give him advice.

It wasn't much of a surprise that Junior also became a **Major League** Baseball player. And what Junior has accomplished in such a short time is simply amazing.

Junior shared his greatest moment in baseball with his father, when they both played on the same **Major League** Baseball team together.

Junior is, without a doubt, one of the best players in the game today. And he constantly gets better. Although he has a lot of natural talent and grew up around the game, he also works hard to be the best baseball player he can be.

He has accomplished more in his first seven years than most players ever do in their entire career.

Ken Griffey, Jr., hits one out.

The Kid

George Kenneth Griffey, Jr., was born on November 21, 1969, in Donora, Pennsylvania. He is the oldest child of Ken and Alberta Griffey. He has one brother, Craig, and a sister, Lathesia.

Senior was just beginning his first season of professional baseball with the Cincinnati Reds' **minor league** team, when Junior was born.

By 1973, Senior made it to the **Major Leagues**. He moved the family to a large house outside Cincinnati. Junior would go to "work" with his dad and swing the bat. When Junior was only five, he knew that he wanted to be a baseball player. He loved the fans and the huge **stadium**. And he was more talented than most kids twice his age.

Senior quickly became a great player for a great team. "The Big Red Machine" won six **National League** West Division titles and the **World Series** in 1975 and 1976.

Junior loved the excitement of the game, especially when they were winning. But he was determined to feel that excitement firsthand. He knew that he wanted to play pro baseball, just like his dad.

And he was well on his way. At the age of 10, while playing **Little League**, Junior got a hit every time he came up to bat. And he had a pitching **record** of 12 wins and no losses.

Ken Griffey, Sr., accepts the Most Valuable Player Award from Commissioner Bowie Kuhn.

Junior Impresses the All-Stars

In 1981, Senior was traded to the New York Yankees. It was very hard on Junior, who was only 12, because he was so close to his father. Only Senior moved to New York, because he wanted to keep his family in one spot and not move them.

On many occasions Junior would go out to New York to visit his father. Before games Junior would take batting practice with his father and the other Yankees. The other players couldn't believe his swing. **All-Star** outfielder Rickey Henderson said he was worried about losing his job to this "kid."

By the age of 15, Junior could swing, throw, run, and catch as well as many **minor leaguers**. His dad, who was also an All-Star, was just as impressed. Because Senior was away from home so much during the summer he never really had the chance to see Junior mature into a great baseball player.

Rickey Henderson knew someday that Junior would be a star in baseball and often gave him advice. Junior idolized Henderson and listened to him. Junior hoped Henderson was right, that someday he would play in the **Major Leagues**.

Father and son—Ken Griffey, Sr., (R) and Ken Griffey, Jr., (L)—made a guest appearance on the 1990 TV show "Harry and the Hendersons."

High School Star

When Junior attended Archbishop Moeller High School, he believed that he would be the star on the baseball team his freshman year. But that didn't happen. In fact, Junior didn't even get to play his first year because of his bad grades.

Junior was smart, but he neglected his school work to play baseball. So Junior had to sit out that first year and watch, which frustrated him.

In his next season Junior didn't play either—not because of his grades, but because he had gone to Florida for **spring training** with his father. He thought that he would get much more baseball practice in Florida than in Ohio. He also loved the idea of spending time with his father.

Finally, in his third year of high school, Junior began to play baseball. Some wondered if it would be too late for him to make an impact and reach the Majors.

It didn't take long to see that the layoff hadn't hurt him at all. He batted .478 and had 11 home runs. He was also the star **wide receiver** on the football team. Colleges were looking at him for football too. But he made it very clear his senior year, when he didn't play high school football, that he certainly wasn't going to play college football either.

But he certainly played baseball his senior year. In fact, his coach called him the best athlete he had ever seen. Junior finished his two-year career in high school, hitting .480, with 20 home runs, a school **record**. Junior was also amazing in the outfield, catching long fly balls while running full speed with his back to home plate!

More important, Junior was making such a name for himself that crowds of **Major League scouts** were watching him play. He never felt pressure from the scouts. He just continued to have fun and play the game that he loved.

Number One Pick

Major League Baseball teams couldn't stop talking about this talented "kid." Five pro **scouts** graded Junior's baseball talents, and each one gave him a score between 63 and 73. A score between 50 and 59 meant that a player was a potential **All-Star**!

Every team wanted him, but they all knew that the number one pick would get him, and that happened to be the Seattle Mariners. On June 2, 1987, when Junior was only 17, the Mariners made him the first pick in the Major League **draft**.

After signing a minor league **contract** that paid him a **bonus** of $160,000, the Mariners were hoping he would be in the Majors within three years.

Many players, especially players who begin so young, stay in the minors at least five years before entering the Majors. But because of his speed, power, and great arm, many thought that Junior could get to the Major Leagues in a lot less time.

Ken Griffey, Jr., hits a double the first time at bat in Major League Baseball.

THE MAKING OF AN AWESOME ATHLETE

Ken Griffey, Jr., (left) and his father (right) made baseball history.

1969	1987	1989	1990
Born November 21 in Donora, Pennsylvania.	Graduates from high school; drafted number one by the Seattle Mariners and is sent to the minor leagues.	The Griffeys become the first father-son combination to play in the Major Leagues as Jr. doubles in his first at-bat.	Becomes the first Mariner to start in the All-Star game; wins his first Gold Glove Award.

How Awesome Is He?

In 1993, Griffey knocked in over 100 runs for the third-straight year. Only four other players in Major League history have matched that feat at an earlier age:

Player	Age	Years
Mel Ott	22	1929-31
Ty Cobb	22	1907-09
Ted Williams	23	1939-41
Joe DiMaggio	23	1936-38
Ken Griffey, Jr.	**23**	**1991-93**

KEN GRIFFEY, JR.

TEAM: SEATTLE MARINERS
NUMBER: 24
POSITION: CENTER FIELD
HEIGHT: 6 FEET 3 INCHES
WEIGHT: 205 LBS.

1992	1993	1994	1995
Named the All-Star MVP.	Sets team records for home runs and RBIs.	Becomes the first Mariner to win the AL home run title.	Leads the Mariners to the playoffs for the first time in team history.

- **1994 Home Run Leader**
- **6-Time Gold Glove Winner**
- **6-Time AL All-Star Selection**
- **1992 All-Star Game MVP**
- **Record-95 Straight Errorless Games in 1990**
- **Homers in Record-Tying 8 Straight Games (1993)**

Highlights

Rocky Times in the Minors

After Junior graduated from high school in 1987, he reported to the Mariners' **rookie minor league**, 80 miles north of Seattle. It was a huge adjustment for Junior, who had lived in a beautiful house with a swimming pool. Now he was living on the road, in old, rundown motels.

Junior did not like that first year of baseball and many times thought about quitting. He missed his family, friends, and the great life he had back home. He started calling home so much that his phone bill was over $600 every month.

Junior was not playing well, either. Experts thought he would be a star, but he wasn't living up to it. Critics thought Junior didn't care.

Finally his mother came out to see him and told him that he had to grow up and concentrate on his career. Junior agreed, and began playing much better.

But after the season, things again went downhill. Junior began feeling **depressed** and **pressured**. In January 1988, Junior tried to kill himself by overdosing on over-the-counter medication. Fortunately, he was rushed to the hospital in time to save his life.

Junior explained that he was depressed, angry, pressured, and upset at the world. He said that trying to commit suicide was a dumb thing, and he made it very clear that it was not the way to solve problems. His father and the rest of his family helped him get through it. Now he was ready once more to concentrate on baseball.

Getting Better

The next season for Junior was much better, both on and off the field. He was now playing in the class A **minor league** with players who were older than he was. But by the middle of the season he was the star attraction. People, especially kids, would come to the games just to see him play.

His dad, who was still playing in the **Majors**, got a chance to see his son play. Senior was so impressed with his son's hitting, running, throwing, and fielding, he told his wife that it didn't make sense for anyone to have that much talent.

Junior was playing great ball. After 58 games, he was batting .338 with 42 **RBIs**, and leading the league in home runs with 11, and **stolen bases** with 32. Then he got hurt and missed most of the remaining season. Even with the shortened season, people got the chance to see Junior's potential.

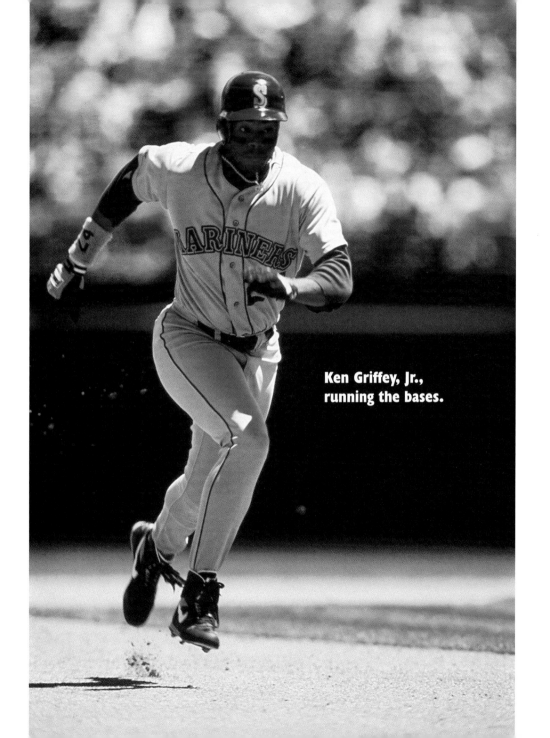

Ken Griffey, Jr.,
running the bases.

Father and Son Make History

In 1989, Junior was hoping to finally get a chance to play in the **Majors**. He began **spring training** playing very well. In 26 spring training games he batted .359. He set team **records** with 33 hits and 21 **RBIs**. To top it off he was playing great defense.

On March 29, the Mariners' **manager,** Jim Lefebvre, told Junior that he had made the team and would now be playing in the Majors. Junior was only 19 years old!

Senior was now 39 years old and trying to make the Reds at his own spring training. After batting .333, there was no doubt that he would make the team. The Griffeys were about to make history as the first father and son combination to play in the **Major Leagues** at the same time.

On April 3, Senior and the Reds played the Dodgers. Senior played but did not get a hit. Later that day Junior and the Mariners played the A's. Junior got a double in

his first at-bat. Senior got to see it on television and
began to cry. Senior was happy for his son. The Griffeys
had made history.

Junior finished his first season in the **Majors** with 16
home runs. He broke a team **record** by reaching base
11-straight times.

The Griffeys, father and son, are interviewed for television.

More History

The next season was even more special for the Griffeys. Senior signed a **contract** in the middle of the season with the Seattle Mariners. Father and son were now making history again, this time because they were going to play on the same team.

On August 31, 1990, Junior and Senior played in their first game together. Senior was up first and hit a smash through the middle of the infield for a single. Junior followed his father up to bat and also hit a single. The crowd went wild. Both balls were collected and taken to the **Baseball Hall of Fame**.

The Griffeys scored runs that inning for the Mariners. When Junior reached the dugout, he was greeted by his father who gave him a big hug.

Besides making history, Junior also hit .300, with 22 home runs. He became the first Mariner voted to start in the **All-Star Game**, and he also won a **Gold Glove Award** that year.

Ken Griffey, Jr., (L) celebrates with teammate, Harold Reynolds, after winning the Gold Glove Award.

MVP

In 1991, Junior continued to improve. He hit .327 and had 100 **RBIs**. He won his second-straight **Gold Glove Award**, and made his second-straight start in the **All-Star Game**. On the defensive side he was voted by the **managers** as the best fielding outfielder in the American league.

Although his team was not playing that well, Junior was. In the 1992 season, he again batted more than .300. He finished with 27 home runs and 103 RBIs.

He also made the All-Star team for the third-straight year. He had a great game, hitting a home run and was named the **Most Valuable Player (MVP)**.

Opposite page: Ken Griffey, Jr., acknowledges a cheering crowd in Seattle after accepting the team's Most Valuable Player Award, 1993.

Bad Timing

Junior's 1993 and 1994 seasons were excellent. In 1993, he tied a **Major League record** by hitting home runs in eight-straight games. He finished the season again batting more than .300 and hit 45 home runs!

He became one of only five players ever to have 100 or more **RBIs** before their 24th birthday.

In 1994, he was on a record pace. By August 11, he already had 40 home runs and 90 RBIs! But, unfortunately, the next day the players went on strike and the season was canceled.

Opposite page: Ken Griffey, Jr., steals third base against the New York Yankees.

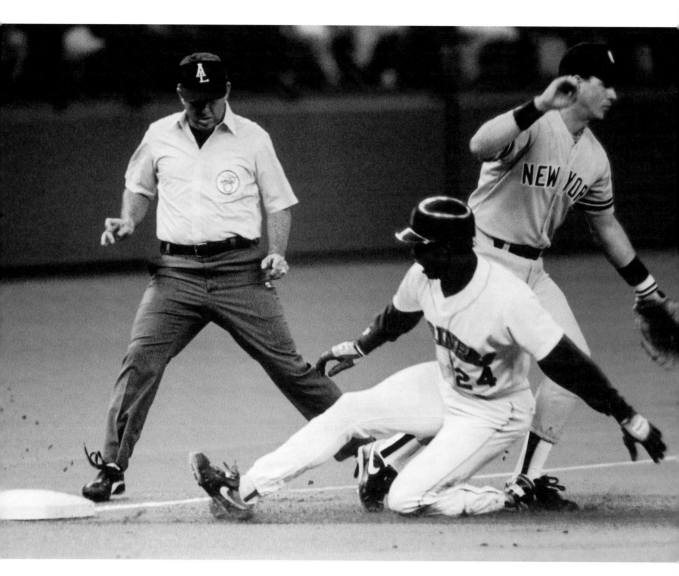

Finally, the Playoffs

In the 1995 season, Junior was often injured and only played in 72 games. But when he played he really helped the team. Along with strong pitching, the Mariners finally made the playoffs for the first time in team history.

The Mariners won the American League West title over the California Angels in a one-game playoff. In the playoffs, Junior was healthy and played in all the games.

In the first round of the playoffs, the Mariners surprised the heavily-favored New York Yankees in a five-game series, winning three games to two.

In the American League Championship against the Cleveland Indians, the Mariners played well but lost some close games. They ended up losing the series four games to two. Junior played well in the playoffs, hitting .333.

Junior Keeps Working

Junior has accomplished a great deal in baseball. He has hit .300 or better in five seasons. He has had 100 or more **RBIs** 3 times and 20 or more home runs 5 times, including 40 or more home runs twice!

His biggest accomplishment, though, was playing alongside his father. Junior feels this way because his father was the person he always looked up to and wanted to be like. And his father is the first to admit that his son is even better at the game than he was.

Junior loves the game and continues to work to be the best player he can be. Someday he would like to win a **World Series** just as his father did. But he doesn't worry about that part very much. He just thinks that he is the luckiest person in the world for being able to play the game he loves, and having a great family to support him all the way.

GLOSSARY

All-Star - A player who is voted by the fans as the best player at one position in a given year.

All-Star Game - A game between the best players in the American and National leagues voted on by the fans.

Baseball Hall of Fame - A memorial for the greatest players of all time located in Cooperstown, New York.

bonus - Extra money paid to a player after signing a contract.

contract - A legal document signed by players that states how much money they will get paid and how many years they will play for a particular team.

depressed - To feel sad or gloomy about your life.

draft - An event held where Major League Baseball teams choose high school or college players to be on their team. The worst team gets the first pick.

Gold Glove Award - An award given to the best defensive players at their positions.

historic - A famous or important event in history that has never taken place before.

Little League - A baseball league for children ranging in the ages between 9 and 12.

Major League - The highest ranking of professional baseball teams in the world, consisting of the American and National Leagues.

manager - The person in charge who makes all of the decisions dealing with a baseball team on the field.

minor league - Three classes and a rookie league of professional baseball at levels below the Major League.

Most Valuable Player (MVP) - An award given to the best player in the league, All-Star Game, or World Series.

National League - An association of baseball teams which make up one half of the major leagues.

pressured - Having too many expectations put on yourself and feeling stress.

RBI - A baseball statistic standing for runs batted in. Players receive an RBI for each run that scores on their hits.

record - The best it has ever been done in a certain event.

rookie - A first-year player in a sport.

scouts - The people who watch athletes play baseball and determine if they have what it takes to make it at a higher level.

spring training - Where baseball players go for a certain amount of time before the regular season starts to get in shape, both physically and mentally and to play many baseball games.

stadium - A place that has a field for baseball and other events and many seats where fans can come and watch the event.

stolen bases - A play in baseball when a base runner advances to the next base while the pitcher is delivering the pitch.

wide receiver - A player in football whose job is to catch the football.

World Series - The championship of Major League Baseball played between the winners of the National and American League.

Index